Cinephilia for Beginners

Tomás Vega Moralejo

INDEX

FOREWORD

It is called the "seventh art" because cinema arrived later than the six classical ones that the Greeks had called superior arts (those which are enjoyed with the "superior senses" sight and hearing): architecture, sculpture, painting, music, declamation (poetry) and dance. It is, of course, more one of these denominations that has rooted in popular culture than a conclusive qualifying position. In the XVIII century the term "fine arts" started to become popular to name the six superior ones, but eloquence was even included and, no doubt, someone will miss theatre more than cinema as a seventh art, or someone might just prefer to move films from that position.

It was the essay "Manifesto of the Seven Arts", published in 1914, which placed cinema at the seventh art and it seems to have remained there.

Whatever the position is, cinema is an art, a fine art. The dictionary says that art is the human manifestation of free mind and the French André Maurois said that "What is beautiful is what is intelligible without reflection". Don't you find it a beautiful definition, even for art?

There are difficulties in understanding certain artistic manifestations. A Velázquez's painting is intelligible without reflection, it is beautiful without hesitation. But, what about a Picasso's painting? Some are quick to classify it as rubbish, I did it myself a long time ago, rejecting it as authentic art... because it requires reflection, it is not intelligible (beautiful) at first glance.

Guernica, for example, is not les abstract than other Picasso's paintings, but it is more accessible: we know that it is a manifestation of the horrors of the Spanish Civil War; we stop to observe it and we gradually identify things in it, we discover the beauty it hides. It is certainly art.

But, as in everything, there's also fraud in art. I don't think that a pile of sand and other building materials unloaded in a room of a Contemporary Art Museum is art, however much we are told that they want to represent what the museum itself is made of; I would rather say that it is just a way to justify the money paid. There are also films which are not understandable even when they are explained to you, but some use them to pretend they know more than the rest.

I don't want to justify, therefore, that everything that is said to be art it is in fact in the absence of an explanation. I mean, on the contrary, that it is good that art leads to reflection, but to do this it must be intelligible in the first place. A film must be understandable, that is the first thing.

It is clear that what I'm saying still has its complications, because knowledge helps to a better appreciation of things... and ignorance may make us disregard a jewel.

A film of simple entertainment such as "Indiana Jones and the Kingdom of the Crystal Skull" contains a few winks, for example, to some historical events, which will delight the ones who get them and which will probably even bore those who don't notice them.

There are more complex films which need previous knowledge or further analysis... Thus, the fact that we don't understand a film does not necessarily mean that it is not good.

...and now I come to where I was thinking when I started to write this foreword: to recommend this book in order to learn to better appreciate cinema, because a basis is needed for everything... but I feel it is imperative to recommend also a series of documentaries (fifteen of an hour each) which will also then help to enjoy cinema more.

"The Story of Film: An Odyssey", by Mark Cousins. 2011.

It is not commercial propaganda, the thing is that there is nothing like this in documentaries.

They overlook great films such as "Schindler's List" and they dedicate minutes to films of a doubtful reputation, such as "Starship Troopers" to illustrate how to leak certain topics such as politics in a discreet way... but the thing is that in these documentaries the emphasis is placed on the details, on innovation.

As in every work, there will be a certain subjectivity of the author and one may not agree with the real influence of some things he/she tells, and, with some of them, we will even wonder if he/she is pulling our legs, just like certain contemporary art artists, but it is indeed very interesting, and maybe the only opportunity, to take a look at films from places such as Iran or Senegal, which would go unnoticed, but in which cinema also matured.

Watching them (documentaries) is not just enjoying yourselves with them, but we will have given ourselves an overview of cinema forever, which will provide us a greater pleasure when watching films.

Some details which today seem obvious, meant authentic revolutions at the time; for example, moving from fixed shots to camera movements, or introducing time spans in stories with images. We will understand that recording with sound also changed the way of filming, or that it is said that "Citizen Kane" is the best film, not because of the story it tells, but for the innovations it introduced in what we watched and how we watched it. A take with a tilted camera, although we hadn't noticed, emphasises the chaos of the scene... and it sounds silly, but it took years before someone had the idea or dared to show us a tilted image. All in all... let us hope that these documentaries don't get lost.

This book is not, and it is by no means intended to be, as ambitious as that documentary series, but it does want, with brevity and simplicity, to help set the foundations on which a love for the cinema may be built from its knowledge... Then it is up to the reader to become an expert with books which deepen more on each subject of the cinema.

CINEPHILIA FOR BEGINNERS

Cinephilia is the love of cinema.

One is not born with cinephilia: cinephilia is made.

Definitely, one thing is that you like "watching films" and another thing is to be a cinephile.

You won't hear a cinephile saying that he/she doesn't want to watch a film just because it is from many years ago, or even in black and white and/or silent.

In order to be a cinephile you have to watch a lot of films, and even examine somewhat what lies beyond the screen: how tough it is to achieve some things which seem very simple when we watch them.

Many people limit themselves to watch "what is coming out", especially when associated to a good marketing campaign, and they even fear films apparently as serious as usually are those winners of various cinema awards. Certainly, great films are lost along the way.

Of course everyone has his/her personal tastes, but in order to form an opinion regarding cinephilia, one has to have culture about cinema; a lot of films have to be watched, among which classics are a must, something more than those films which only seek to be a blockbuster.

Then, whether they are liked or not depends on everyone, but, if we don't watch them, we will lack those points of reference on the basis of which the rest may be judged in a more objective way. Classics must be watched, and I encourage you to have a look at the "how it was made" of some films. This way one learns to better appreciate this art.

Cinema as a school:

Our personality is forged around a genetic basis, the education given by our relatives and nearest ones, and our teachers... and also around our experiences. Who hasn't been taught anything by cinema? Who hasn't been touched deeply by a film?

A renowned film critic said that, with "Schindler´s List", Spielberg had managed to make our feelings go through memorable moments. And I truly believe that this great film, from 1993, but in black and white, is the best way to teach the absurdity and awfulness of Nazism. I do not believe there is a high school lesson, speech, documentary... which could be able to make the horrors of war as clear as this film, which does not belong, however, to a war genre. The end is so moving that one has the feeling that something more than crying is needed to cope with it.

Other films make us think about things we probably hadn't even noticed, although they were always there.

"It's a Wonderful Life", by Frank Capra, might be over sweetened, but it makes us reflect on our time in the world and how we influence others and others influence us... and it encourages us to be become better people. Or what about the "magic" of Disney films? Walt Disney should have received the Nobel Peace Prize, although while living nobody could assess of his legacy, which goes beyond cinephilia. I am sure that the increasing awareness of society towards values, such as respect for animals, owes a lot to the world of Disney.

In the opposite direction, films such as "Saw" come to my mind. Can anything positive emerge out of such sadism? Such films may serve as an inspiration for disturbed minds. I don't understand, then, the controversy for having given the "X" rating to one of the films of the saga; the controversy should be in why the previous ones were not also rated like that... or even in why such kind of films are made and/or allowed. I know that what I have just pointed out may seem to go against the freedom of the creator and the viewer, but it is not enough even with the film age ratings, as it remains as a mere recommendation which anyone can let pass; especially now, with the internet.

By the way, talking about the internet: a cinephile does not watch a film any which way, because a film illegally downloaded, with a poor quality of image and/or sound, is like eating a raw potato... as well as a fraud, which is truly unfair, for the number of people who, directly or indirectly, have worked in a film and make a living out of it.

Watching cinema:

We've talked about what films to watch and why. We've even approached how much and when: as much as we can and, if it's possible, at the cinema, but if not, wherever you like, as long as it's not pirated.
How and when to watch it is also important... and even with whom.

Should a funny film be watched when we're really sad? We won't probably be amused. Our circumstances weigh on to what extent the film is going to please us, not to mention that age, for example, has also influence (it is not the same to watch "E.T.: The Extra-Terrestrial" with 7 years than with 17), or our past experiences and even our culture or intelligence in understanding and being able to better appreciate certain films.

Empathy also has an impact. If, for example, we're watching a comedy with someone who is not keen on the wittiness of the film, that will restrain us in such a way that it will be less likely that we laugh and enjoy ourselves.

With all this what happens is that judging a film is something subjective, not just because your own judgement is personal, but because not even ourselves always have the same opinion. Professional film critics themselves allow themselves great subjectivities. Nevertheless, in order to have our opinion respected, we should know about cinema... and, in order to know about cinema, you have to watch a lot of films and also have some basis of its history and some concepts. And we're working on it in this book, I hope you find its reading enjoyable and rewarding.

And who am I to give advice on cinema? Well... I've watched thousands of films and dozens of documentaries and I've read dozens of works about cinema; I am among those who stays up all night, here in Spain, to watch the Oscar ceremonies and I've even done some first steps with filming, but, in the end, I'm only a cinephile to whom you should pay no more attention than what you wish: actually, the same as to a film critic, who, after all, dedicate themselves to express personal opinions about films... and that is right for us, because it's good to have references of what is going to be watched or contrast opinions.

A BRIEF HISTORY OF CINEMA

The History of Cinema allows for an encyclopaedia, but this is Cinephilia for Beginners: Let's run through cinema from its origins until the present day in less than 2500 words.

The background of cinema is to be found in photography, whose beginning might be set in **1839**, when the French Louis J. M. Daguerre promoted the development of the **daguerreotype**, the first photographic process through which an image could be fixed on a copper plate which reacted to the light. The method was improved with silver salts and, in parallel, new systems with pictures became available, which, when rotating, gave a sense of animation.

The combination of photography and rotating devices are, indeed, the background of cinema:
In **1879** the English Edward Muybridge captured his photos on a transparent circular plate which he placed inside a projector called zoopraxiscope, resulting in the **first realistic images in motion** (a jockey and his galloping horse).

Émile Reynaud improved on the zoopraxiscope and on 28 October 1892 he projected what is considered the mother work of animated cinema: Pantomimes Lumineuses.

William Kennedy Laurie Dickson, a Scotsman who worked for Thomas Alva Edison, designed the first film studio and allowed the **kinematograph** to be patented, which pulled the flexible strips of Kodak founder George A. Eastman's perforated celluloid. They also created the kinetoscope, a sort of box with a peephole for an individual projection; it projected around 800 images for about 20 seconds. We are **at the end of the XIX century**; the first kinetoscope hall was opened on 14 August 1894.

(Edison attributed some inventions to himself for being the first one to patent them, but in the case in question he didn't do it in Europe)

The next step would be a **cinematograph** for screen projections for the audience, and now we come to the birth of cinema as such... choose a date, because there's no unanimous agreement:

On 13 February 1895, the Lumière brothers Auguste and Louis registered the patent of the cinematograph, and on **22 March 1895**, they presented "**Workers Leaving The Lumière Factory in Lyon**", lasting 46 seconds.

On 10 June 1895, they exhibited for the first time "The Waterer Watered" in a basement in Paris, the first film (although it only lasted 49 seconds) with a plot in history, with the first paid actor: Lumière brothers' gardener.

The first public exhibition of 12 films, which added up to half an hour, with paid admission, was made on 28 December 1895, in the "Indian Hall of Grand Café", in Paris, with an announcement on a poster.

Around 1900, George Albert Smith and others started to use the camera going beyond the fixed shots and this one, in addition, invented the kinemacolor, the first coloured film process with some success.

Until then, the cinema was basically dedicated to show the reality. Charles Pathé, for example, created the first newsreel and, along with his brothers, he founded the first film production company.

Georges Méliès pioneered fiction, and with the 14 minutes and 12 seconds of his "A Trip to the Moon " (1902), he marked a before and after. With a cost of 30,000 francs, it can also be considered the first blockbuster.

Edwin S. Porter added innovations in editing and narration in "Life of an American Fireman".

Cinema had ceased to be a visual curiosity to become art.
Companies began to organise themselves into channels of production, distribution and exhibition. It was calculated in 1908 that there were around 14 million viewers per week in US "**nickelodeons**", screening rooms for the price of one nickel (5 cents).

Edison joined producers and distributors to form the "Motion Picture Patents Company" and then almost fully control the market, which caused the so-called "**patent

war": those who wanted to use film equipment and projections under patent had to pay. Some independent producers, such as the German Carl Laemmle, faced Edison and the monopoly was dissolved in 1912, but it had already brought about the movements which would lead to shift the film industry to the West (far from the influence of the "Motion Picture Patents Company") and to the establishment of the large film companies.

Laemmle himself founded in 1912 Universal Studios and, later on, Adolph Zukor (from Hungary) founded Paramount, William Fox did the same with Fox, Samuel Goldwyn founded Goldwyn and Jack L. Warner established, along with his brothers Harry, Albert and Sam, the Warner Bros.

Most companies gradually settled, then, in **Hollywood**, on some sunny areas near Los Angeles, acquired in 1887 by the Wilcox couple.

Once the industrial bases had been established, it was time to put the emphasis on improving the artistic ones.

David Wark Griffith excelled at it, and " The Birth of a Nation" is, with regards to what it says, a despicable racist film, but it marked a before and after regarding **cinematographic narrative**: more shots, near, far, camera movement... whereas the cinema in Europe was still quite similar to the theatre, even though different artistical trends gradually emerged, such as impressionism or expressionism and the documentary cinema.

Unfortunately, the convulsive environment in Europe at the time made many European talented filmmakers emigrate to Hollywood.

We're around the year 1920, with more than a hundred thousand workers for the film studios, from where around a thousand films came out per year.

The film business gradually focused more on the so-called "**star-system**", where productions were custom-made for the film star actors and actresses, who became mass idols.
Two of these stars, besides being a couple, Douglas Fairbanks and Mary Pickford, had created another of the emblematic studios, in association with Griffith and Charles Chaplin: United Artists.

The producer Louis B. Mayer suggested the creation of an **Academy of Motion Picture Arts and Sciences in Hollywood**, and this was founded in **1927** with Douglas Fairbanks as the first president.
In **1931** they would create **the Oscars**... but we will talk about that in a different chapter of this book.

Lee De Forest, already in 1923, had a way to register **sound** and image simultaneously, but that meant changing the way of making films and the studios were reluctant... until the Warner developed its own system, the Vitaphone, which registered sound separately but it was then synchronised.
On 6 August 1926, "Don Juan" was presented as the first film in history with its own sound; and on 6 October 1927 "The Jazz Singer" was released, with human voice

for the first time.

By the end of **1929** Movietone would improve the system and silent films would be sentenced, although films in silent and sound versions were still made for some years, allowing time for the adaptation of the exhibition halls and the industry in general. In the meantime, films in different language versions were made, even changing the actors.

The cost for the producers was important in that process of change, which, by the mid-1930s was fully established, but some actors and actresses were affected in another sense, as they didn't know how or were not able to adapt themselves to the sound film.

Regarding the establishment of **colour**, Herbert T. Kalmus had already patented the Technicolor system already in 1915, but its complexity and even imperfection, and the fact that the establishment of sound film had already been considered for some time scourge enough for the cinema, left the popularisation of colour for around the 40s.

With the cinema in good moments, certain excesses for those times had also arrived: such as the trivialisation of infidelity or alcohol in films; and fears were raised about the bad influence of cinema in society. That way, the Hays Code for **censorship** was established in 1930, bearing the surname of the Republican who wrote it.

In 1930 eight **major companies** controlled the industry almost entirely, being the first five the ones with the greatest weight: Paramount (Created in 1914 by William W. Hodkinson), Metro Goldwyn Mayer (1924, when merging Metro Pictures [founded in 1915 by Richard A. Rowland], Goldwyn Pictures [1917] and Louis B. Mayer Pictures [1918]), Fox (1915, by William Fox; it merged in 1935 with The Twentieth Century by Darryl Zanuck, created two years before), Warner Bros (1923), RKO (1928, Radio Keith Orpheum), Columbia (1919, by Harry Cohn), United Artists (1919) and Universal (1912, as we have said before).

Walt Disney started gaining share in 1937 with "Snow White and the Seven Dwarfs", the first full-length animated feature film.

Cinematographic genres (adventure, crime, horror, ...) gradually settled and the musical enjoyed great success, to the extent that, for a period of time, almost every film included some songs.

Europe lagged behind US, and the outbreak of the **Second World War** made things worse and it also left a mark on cinema, as could not have been otherwise. Among other things, film production was drastically reduced and it affected its content, in such a way that, frequently, even non-war films appealed to the patriotic feeling or reflected the evil of the enemy.

There was also place, of course, for films that sook to escape from reality, but **neorealism** gained strength after the war: showing pure and simple reality; particularly in Italy.

By the end of the 1940s, cinema forgot the Nazis and communists became the meanest in US.

The Cold War, with the fear of another real war, affected the cinema to the point of making many leading figures of this art end up in prison or without a job, accused of being "anti-American" for being communists... and the "**witch-hunt**" meant a chaos because of the accusations or defences from one another, which put an end to the golden age of cinema, capped with the advent of television to the homes.

The response of the industry to **television** was enlarging the projection screens and creating spectacular films such as Ben-Hur; and the reaction was good, but the problem is that the massive production of films with such characteristics was not possible...

At the same time in India (Raj Kapoor, Satyajit Ray) or in Mexico (Cantinflas), **national** cinema was in good health, but in contrast to what happened in the US cinema, it hardly had any international projection. Great Britain did gradually gain access and, at a certain distance, France (Cocteau, Tati), Italy (Rossellini, Visconti, Fellini), the Scandinavian countries (Ingmar Bergman) or even Japan (Akira Kurosawa).

Regarding Spain, in the midst of the Franco dictatorship, there's barely any remarkable film and even some major filmmakers, such as Luis Buñuel, were in exile.

By the end of the 1950s, the major studios, added to the

problem of television, saw: antitrust laws, the dispersal of the population to towns where there were no cinema halls... and many actors chose to produce themselves, although, sometimes, with some support from the major production companies, which finally ended up selling their previous films to televisions and making new low-budget ones, or series directly for television, so their great enemy ended up being their salvation at the time.

It was time in the 70s to renovate the classical genres, already very predictable, and an **auteur cinema** emerged with force ("nouvelle vague" included), arthouse or experimental film (without forgetting the "underground" film). Violence began to be shown with greater realism and the ends of the films were no longer always happy.

Co-productions among countries became a trend and Spain and Italy were common sets to shoot. It was the time of the "peplum" or "Roman films" and the "spaghetti-western", in particular, by Sergio Leone. Erotic cinema also became fashionable, until porn cinema was born in 1972 with "Deep Throat", although it is not usually taken into account as authentic cinema, among other things, because its actors and actresses do not even perform, as the sex act is not simulated.

Also in the seventies, many European actors competed with those from Hollywood for fame, and **European cinema** managed to put aside that of US... until the arrival of Spielberg, Coppola, Lucas and Scorsese, among others, in addition to the boom of special effects.

Those were good times for science fiction, for adventure films and also horror cinema.

In addition to the countries already established in cinema, Australia would also show itself to the world and it would be the zenith of the Japanese Akira Kurosawa.

The **Betamax** system, by Sony, arrived in 1975 and, soon after, that of **VHS**, by JVC, which would work things out better and would end up prevailing as a home video tape.
The decade of the 80s was the boom of the videotape. At the beginning, everything was business: films were released at the cinema, then in videotapes and afterwards in television; **video shops** and revival halls were born… but in the end that meant the closure of many cinemas and the industry had to respond with multi-screen cinemas, a better sound, better seats….

Continuing with the eighties: it was the time of muscular tough guys such as Stallone, Schwarzenegger, Chuck Norris, Bruce Willis, ….

We arrive to the nineties and to the **digital revolution**, which could be said to have begun with "Terminator 2" (1991), by James Cameron, and another notable leap forward in 1993 with "Jurassic Park", by Steven Spielberg, or, in another sense, "Toy Story" (1995) by Pixar, the first film to be completely computer generated.

It was also the decade where, finally women gradually took their place in cinema, with outstanding films for and by women.

The digitalisation of cinema, also in terms of the format itself in which it was recorded, has brought about great changes in distribution and other fronts... almost all good, but it has also made piracy easier, which is shown as the greatest danger for cinema by causing it multi-million losses.

In the first decade of the 21st century, the sagas which split films into parts dependent on each other multiplied, something seemingly contrary to the essence of cinema but that, with "Harry Potter" or "The Lord of the Rings", meant a good way to keep on taking advantage of cinemas.

In recent years **technical developments** have carried on, such as motion capture and 3D perfected by the film "Avatar", and shortly after 4K and 4D, ...

The possibility of doing everything digitally is probably near.
The last boundary is to make human movement natural, especially with regard to facial expression... Will actors and actresses be necessary in cinema in the **future**?

<u>WHO IS WHO? – *How a film is made*</u>

By paying attention to the credit titles, which should not be missed by a good cinephile, because a film does not really end until these are over (moreover, sometimes they embed surprises such outtakes), we see that there are dozens or hundreds of people who make a film possible, who, as a person or as a group, have their specific function... and that is what we're going to deal with now, but without turning this section into just an English dictionary.

A film is born out of an **idea**... and usually the first step is to have it on a **script**, whether it be original or adapted from a pre-existing work.

The **producer** is the owner of the film.
He/She is often present, and can make decisions throughout the creation process: from pre-production (script contract, etc.) up to post-production (editing, adding the soundtrack, ...), including, of course, shooting.
In the past, the producer usually put the money from his/her own pocket. Nowadays, in general, we could say that he/she is the one who manages to get the money, although not necessarily his/hers (especially in Europe there is often state aid to protect its own cinema).
The producer, as we will see with other major people in charge of a film, may delegate tasks or have assistants.

The **executive producer** is usually in charge of seeking funding, administering and spending it.

The producer chooses and contracts a **director**, whom he/she will meet to decide about the actors participating in the film, locations where to shoot, etc... and before starting to shoot, there will be meetings particularly in between the director and each one of the departments involved in the film.

The director may have planned the script on a technical one, where it is decided how to record the scenes.

During the shooting, the burden of the decisions will fall on him, and even after the shooting, he will supervise the editing of the film.

For all those reasons the director is also often called "filmmaker" and "a film by" is usually applied to him/her...", although, of course, many people will have had their influence on the result and, in fact, strictly speaking, the owner of the film is the producer.

If there is a **production manager**, it is him/her who plans the shooting.

The **director's assistant** prepares and coordinates whatever is necessary to shoot, such as the material and actors needed for each take, or takes care, for example, of the secondary aspects of the takes, such as the direction of the extras in a scene.

The second assistant, or **second assistant director**, helps the first one..., for example, by diverting pedestrians from a place if that is required for a take.

The **script supervisor**, mainly done by women, supervises how each take is carried out with regard to the original idea, the duration of each scene, the order of the shots, the changes that have taken place and other matters which may be of importance if, for example, a take has to be repeated. He/she is, somewhat, the director's right hand. An important task of the script supervisor is to oversee the continuity between sequences and prevent from happening things like, for example, a drastic change of time in each shot if there is a clock in the background.

Sometimes there are second unit directions, for example, to shoot a battle if the main director does not particularly like it or is not particularly good at that type of scene.

The **filmmaker** is in charge of the "location" of the film, that is, choosing the places where it will be shot.

The production director at this point should be resolving administrative procedures, such as shoot permits or insurances.

Although the main cast is mainly the responsibility of the producer and the director, the cast in general is an issue of the **production executive**.

Regarding the cast, the figure of the recruiter should also be remembered, whose focus was to explore cities searching among students, theatre actors, models, etc..

Subsequently, these would become casting directors or artistic **agents** or representatives, which is the currently prevailing figure and there are agencies which even control productions by determining who would participate in them.

Actors and actresses are the most visible figures in a film and there's only need to mention that they may be leading, secondary ones, extras or bit players... including cameos (a term, by the way, coined by the producer Mike Todd when he prepared "Around the World in 80 Days").

Stunt performers:
Stand-ins, to stay instead of the actor while the lighting is prepared. Body doubles, to substitute an actor, for example, in erotic scenes. Action doubles, to substitute an actor in risky scenes (this began to be carried out in 1903, in the film " The Great Train Robbery").

The **clapperboard** is an emblematic object in cinema, and it has a very important function, as it contains information of each scene, essential for the order and later editing: number or name of the sequence, shot and take, to catalogue them. Its "scissors" serve to, when doing *"clack"*, synchronise image and sound, as they are usually recorded separately.

Director of photography, also known as first **operator** or chief operator: he/she controls the light. The actual operator is at his/her orders, who is often the one who takes the camera and does the framing and movements of the camera.

The **first assistant camera** or focus puller constantly measures the distance between the lens of the camera and the elements to be focused, for a perfect focus.

The second assistant camera helps in whatever is needed with it.

The **video assistant** carries an auxiliary camera system so that the director may check how the takes look like.

The **still photographer** takes pictures of relevant moments during the shooting.

The gaffer is the *lighting technician*.

The generator operator takes care of the mobile generator set when it is needed.

The **construction grips** (the leader is called *key grip*) mount and handle the camera mobile supports, such as the cranes.

The **custom designer** does not need so much explaining, as the name itself indicates what he/she does; he/she has the custom design assistant, who is the one supervising the dressmaking. Different tailors work for them, some of whom will also be present during the shooting in case, for example, the actor's piece of clothing has a loose button.

Although they are not widely known people, they create fashion.

Art directors lead the visual and artistic aspects. In the past, painted sets used to be common, later on, they added more or less complete reconstructions of the places they wanted to shoot... to end up mainly in real locations. Depending on the film, a combination of elements is used, to which a blue-green background was recently added, to lay images on it or digital effects afterwards (Chroma Key).

The art director is responsible for the **set designers** and prop masters. The **prop buyer** is responsible for sourcing props.

The **production designer** is in charge of choosing the sets or backgrounds where shooting takes place.

The **key makeup artist** designs the characterisation of the characters. He/She has assistants, including hairdressing.

The sound director or **sound operator** is responsible for the boom operator.

Editing teams, special effects teams, technical consultants for specific issues... and even media relations directors, accountants, lawyers, drivers, etc complete the staff needed to make a film.

We've been going deep into more technical aspects of how a film is made, we don't forget something intrinsic to humanity, such as mistakes... in cinema: for example, TV format changes which make the sides of something originally recorded as panoramic disappear (the standard negative was 35 mm); or the common one of the boom operator, who has to follow the actors with the microphone in the air and, at the slightest distraction, the microphone might be shown in the film; or anachronisms, such as showing a wristwatch in a Roman film.

The scenes are usually shot in a way that is considered the most practical and/or cost-effective, not necessarily in chronological order, so it is the **editor**'s job to put them in order, but also to set the pace of the film.

The special effects may be just the darkening of the image so that something that is recorded during the day appears to be night. If a film needs a lot of special effects, already during the shooting there's usually a **special effects supervisor** to plan scenes in order to add those special effects afterwards. The presence of special effects team members is also usually required directly in the shooting, for example, if artificial fog, rain or controlled fire have to be added to a scene. There are even effects which have to be planned well in advance, such as the inclusion of decorative paints which, for example, give an effect of depth to a scene.
Nevertheless, all that has many times been substituted by digital image synthesis, and pioneering tricks, such as that of the 60 cm King Kong which pretended to be a giant in the 1933 film, are now history.
Other major progresses in special effects, already more recent and of a gradually less technical nature, were

seen in "2001: A Space Odyssey", "Terminator 2", "Jurassic Park" or "Avatar".

Regarding the sound, in the decade of the 1930s the optical soundtrack was definitely implemented to the image edge, putting an end to the "silent film era", although it was actually common from the beginning to have even orchestras at the screening of silent films (by the way, talking about orchestras, I recommend you to attend any of the fantastic concerts given by the Film Symphony Orchestra, a Spanish pioneering symphonic orchestra, specialised in film music) and people playing sounds at certain times of the film. Digital sound would arrive at a later stage, with breakthroughs such as the Dolby, DTS, THX, …… but let's deal with the people who are responsible for the sound:

The head of **sound** and his/her assistant record it live.

The sound designer will take care of everything that has to do with it, from the shooting to the editing, if the sound has a special importance in the film.

There will be a sound effects creator.

There's usually a special sound editor, as it is generally split up into different tracks: at least the dialogue, music and effects. The sound mixer will put the tracks together into a single one.

As for the dubbing in different languages, there's usually a dubbing director, and a dub voice actor for each or even several voices.

The **subtitler** has the difficult task of displaying just around twelve letters per second, so as not to make things too hard for the viewer, therefore the subtitles are not totally faithful to what is said in the film.

The musicians who compose for films heighten or add emotions.

Once the film has been completed, it's time for the distribution. The **distributor** also prepares the launch campaign, marketing, reproduction rights contracts for television and video and even the film titles for other languages different from the original one.
The major distributors manage to condition the exhibitors to give preference to their tapes, and the viewers to watch them (going as far as spending even half of the total budget of the film for its promotion), in such a way that other great films even remain without being released in cinemas.
The distributor will have, among others, its advertising department, for example, to prepare the film trailer and poster, and its press department, to prepare interviews with the main characters of the film and other action so that the film is positively received by the different media, such as the delivery of press kits or press books in the form of scripts or image and/or sound fragments from the film.

The **exhibitor**, that is, the cinema or film theatre, is the final goal of a film, and the profits for the entrance (VAT and other concepts applied in other countries separately) are negotiated between the latter and the distributor, who, in turn, will have to settle accounts with the producer and maybe with the scriptwriter, director, etc. That depends on how the contract has been made, which may be based on the percentage on ticket sales or may have been predetermined regardless of the success. Some countries impose a screen quota on the exhibitors, so as to make room for their own productions, since, otherwise, US productions are the ones that prevail.

The exhibitor may also include advertisements before the projections.

Finally, the exhibitor will only let adults in, in special cinema halls, if the tape has been X-rated... but the rest of age ratings in Spain is merely a guideline... Censorship times, which mutilated many films, are far behind.

Other countries have less permissive systems, and others still maintain censorship. In the US, for example, the ratings are close to the Spanish ones, but, being a more conservative society, when a film is rated for adults, it has a huge impact and that is why productions try to avoid such restrictive age ratings... although, curiously, in the US they are rather puritanical with sex scenes and too permissive with those of violence.

Regarding the **film critic**, I must say that he/she is sometimes dependent on the financial support or the access to material from the film, or even the film itself, from some distributors or production companies or media close to them... in such a way that reviews sometimes certainly *put one over on us*. Then, it is also worth consulting pages where the viewers may vote for films, such as FilmAffinity. Nevertheless, the figure of the film critic is interesting and I don't mean to say with this paragraph that they don't have their importance.

Film festivals are a great opportunity for the debut of a film... in particular for independent films, as the major studios usually organise their own release party for their great productions.

Finally, the awards won by the films in those festivals or other competitions are usually their passport to posterity (not necessarily to commercial success), but cinema is not an exact science... therefore, the awards are also sometimes unfair.

A film usually takes six months to go from cinema to home video, beginning with the rental market (although video shops have almost disappeared) and shortly after with the selling one. There are also the pay and subscription channels. After six more months, films are already usually shown on public television. But all those periods have changed with digital platforms, some of which control their own films, such as Netflix or Disney.

50 CINEMA PERSONALITIES TO FOLLOW (and why)

(NO DOUBT SOME WILL THINK THAT IN THIS LIST THERE ARE THOSE WHO SHOULDN'T BE INCLUDED AND THOSE MISSING BUT, IF YOU TAKE A LOOK AT THE FILMOGRAPHY OF THESE CELEBRITIES, YOU WILL FIND INTERESTING FILMS)

[NOTE: ALTHOUGH IT IS NOT THE PURPOSE OF THIS BOOK, IT IS CURIOUS TO SEE IN MANY CASES THE ACTUAL NAME IN PARTICULAR OF THE INTERPRETERS, WHOM WE USUALLY KNOW BY THEIR ARTISTIC NAMES. I INVITE YOU TO PAY ATTENTION TO THAT WHENEVER YOU HAVE THE CHANCE]

Alan Menken
He's the composer of marvellous music for animation films.

Alfred Hitchcock
He's certainly the master of suspense.

Barbra Streisand
She's a multifaceted woman, breaking marks in the Golden Globe Awards.

Billy Wilder
He's considered one of the best screenwriters, in addition to a great director.

Cary Grant
He's elegance.

Charles Chaplin
He was the creator of silent films and a humour which has not lost its flavour over the years.

Clint Eastwood
He's a quality actor and director, he's the tough guy par excellence; and, since I don't include any Western among the films to follow, I indicate here "Pale Rider", directed and starred by him.

Daniel Day-Lewis
Although he doesn't have a very extensive filmography, his perfection as an actor has left a mark.

David W. Griffith
He modernised the narrative in cinema.

Ennio Morricone
His music is half the film in many films, and some Westerns are not understood without him, but he is, in general, one of the best musicians of all times.

Eric Idle
Monty Python.

Francis Ford Coppola
He's a filmmaker who has to his credit some of the best films.

Frank Capra
It's a Wonderful Life.

George Lucas
His commercial vision and involvement with special effects have given us many good moments.

Harrison Ford
He's one of the most versatile actors.

Ingrid Bergman
She was one of the best film stars.

Jack Nicholson
He's one of the best actors, including peculiar characters that would probably be impossible without him.

James Cameron
He's a spectacular filmmaker and the driving force behind great technical advances.

James Horner
Although he left us too soon, he had enough time to be one of the best soundtrack composers.

James Stewart
He was a great actor, with great films.

Javier Bardem
He's the best Spanish actor and one of the best in the world.

Jennifer Lawrence
She's one of the best actresses... and she's still very young.

Joaquin Phoenix
He's one of the best actors, and there is no character that can resist him, however difficult it might be.

John Ford
He's one of the great directors.

John Lasseter
Pixar.

John Williams
He's the soundtrack composer par excellence.

Katharine Hepburn
She is the interpreter with most Oscars.

Kathleen Kennedy
She's a producer with a very good eye for the cinema.

Kathryn Bigelow
Despite not being very prolific, she's a great filmmaker.

Leonardo Di Caprio
He's the actor of the moment.

Marlon Brando
He's one of the best actors of all times.

Martin Scorsese
He's one of the best directors, and one among those who has best managed to capture violence.

Meryl Streep
She is the best interpreter.

Orson Welles
He's one of the most influential filmmakers.

Quentin Tarantino
He maybe likes to show blood more than he should, but his way of directing has something special.

Ridley Scott
He's a master of science fiction... and more.

Robert De Niro
He's one of the most versatile actors, although some of his last roles were not necessary.

Robert Redford
He's a magnificent actor beyond his fame as a handsome man.

Robert Richardson

He's one of the best cinematographers, something whose importance the audience often does not notice.

Robert Zemeckis

He's a director with special effects.

Roger Deakins

He's another one of the great cinematographers, creator of atmospheres and responsible for making what we watch in films more beautiful and special.

Samuel L. Jackson

Although it is arguable, he's the most influential actor, according to an Italian study trying to apply science to determine it... a curious study, to say the least, published in "Applied Network Science" with information taken from the largest film database on the Internet (IMDb).

Stanley Kubrick

He's the director of perfection.

Steven Spielberg

Is he the best director of all times?

Tim Burton
He's the power to the imagination.

Tom Hanks
He's one of the most important actors.

Vangelis
In my opinion, he's the best musician of all times. Objectively, he's one of the best soundtrack musicians, despite the academy having turned its back on him after he didn't go to pick up his Oscar for "Chariots of Fire"... notwithstanding all the indisputable later works such as "Blade Runner" or "1492: The Conquest of Paradise"..

Walt Disney
He's the animation.

William Wyler
He's the director with the most Oscar nominations.

Woody Allen
He's one of the most prolific and peculiar screenwriters and directors, among other facets.

50 FILMS YOU SHOULD SEE (and why)

(NO DOUBT SOME WILL THINK THAT THERE ARE THOSE WHICH SHOULDN'T BE INCLUDED AND THOSE MISSING... IN PARTICULAR LONG AGO CLASSICS, MANY OF WHICH I HAVE LEFT OUT, BECAUSE I CONSIDER THAT, ALTHOUGH THEY HAD THEIR IMPORTANCE AT THE TIME, THEY HAVE NOT BORN WELL THE PASSING OF TIME)

[I ENCOURAGE YOU, BY THE WAY, TO PAY ATTENTION TO THE TRANSLATIONS-ADAPTATIONS WHICH HAVE BEEN MADE OF THE TITLES TO OTHER LANGUAGES, BECAUSE, IN MANY CASES, WHAT HAS BEEN DONE IS VERY CURIOUS AND EVEN FUNNY. TOGETHER WITH THE MISTAKES IN FILMS, FOR WHICH THERE ARE SPECIALISED BOOKS, IT IS ANOTHER ONE OF THE CINEMA]

12 Angry Men   1957
It's a film almost entirely shot in only one room, but with such a deepness that it could make us change our minds.

2001: A Space Odyssey   1968
Each shot is a work of art and it is, probably, the most influential science fiction film.

All about Eve   1950
14 Oscar nominations must have something behind them.

Avatar 2009
It was the most expensive film at the time, it meant a technological leap for the cinema and it's a pure visual spectacle.

Bambi 1942
It's an everlasting and tender plea for the life of animals, it's a pity some adults forget about it.

Beauty and the Beast 1991
It's a jewel of animation, with at jewel of a soundtrack.

Ben-Hur 1959
It's the greatest blockbuster of historical cinema, with 11 Oscars backing it up.

Big Fish 2003
It's a wonderful tale.

Black Mirror: Men Against Fire 2016
Since there are films which are put in episodes, why not focusing attention on episodes of series in which each one of them is actually a film? Black Mirror is a truly remarkable series in that sense and this "episode" leaves no one indifferent.

Blade Runner   1982
Is it the best science fiction film? [I recommend "The Final Cut" by the director]

Braveheart   1995
It's an epic film.

Cast Away   2000
It's an actor, an incredible film.

Citizen Kane   1941
It's one of those which set the trend and changed the way of making films.

City Lights   1931
It's Charlot combining the best humour with a great story, and the best boxing match in history.

Dumb and Dumber   1994
It's foolish, indeed, but it makes you roar with laughter rather than laugh.

E.T.: The Extra-Terrestrial   1982

It's ETernal.

Ex Machina   2015
It's one of the best films to reflect on artificial intelligence.

Finding Nemo   2003
It's a great story, with Pixar's animated preciousness.

Forrest Gump   1994
"A lucky fool" would be a rough sentence applicable to this film, but yet thinking so, isn't it beautiful?

Frankenweenie   2012
It's a great example of "Stop-Motion", with Tim Burton's imagination.

Gandhi   1982
It's the story of an authentic "Jesus Christ".

Gone with the Wind   1939
It's one of the greatest films in history.

Harry Potter and the Sorcerer's Stone   2001

It's the magic in cinema, in a film which started one of the greatest sagas and possibly even the trend of films in episodes.

It's a Wonderful Life 1946
How would life be without you?

Jaws 1975
It was the film which made us fear water.

Jurassic Park 1993
It's the first (and entertaining) time that dinosaurs seemed not to be extinct.

La La Land 2016
It's a good example of a musical, and one of the films on the podium of the 14 Oscar nominations.

Life Is Beautiful 1997
It's the horrors of war filtered by love.

March of the Penguins 2005
It's a documentary with a story. It's a natural tragedy, with animals which do not know that they're being actors. It's lovely.

Mary Poppins   1964
It's an endearing and everlasting mixture of animation and real images.

Monty Python's Life of Brian   1979
It's Monty Python's humour in its fullest expression.

Okja   2017
It's a great example of that cinema which is not released in cinemas, and, unfortunately, a poor plea for the animals in a film. I suggest going beyond with documentaries such as (in crescendo): Blackfish - The Cove - Dominion - Earthlings

Psycho   1960
It's quality horror.

Saving Private Ryan   1998
The first half hour makes you wonder if Spielberg travelled in time to shoot.

Schindler's list   1993
It's THE FILM.

Secret in Their Eyes   2009
It's a great film made in South America.

Snow White and the Seven Dwarfs   1937
It was the first full-length animated feature film and it is still considered well done more than eighty years later.

Star Wars   1977
It's one of those which has to be watched because it is also a social phenomenon.

The Artist   2011
Who said that black-and-white silent cinema had already passed into history?

The Disaster Artist   2017
Let's watch a bad film (the worst one in history?) inside a good film.

The Godfather   1972
It's Cinema with a capital C.

The Godfather: Part II   1974
It's a second part which proves that second parts are not

always bad.

The Lion King   1994
It's the best animation film.

The Lord of the Rings: The Return of the King   2003
It's a great blockbuster.

The Naked Gun   1988
Leslie Nielsen is in his full swing, in a hilarious film of English humour.

The Sea Inside   2004
It's the right to Live and die with dignity.

The Shawshank Redemption   1994
It's one of the greatest ones.

The Truman Show   1998
It is "Big Brother", but serious.

Titanic   1997
It's spectacular.

Toy Story 1995

It was the first completely digital film, and an animated joy.

A FILM DICTIONARY

In this sort of film dictionary I've tried not to include words or acronyms whose meaning I consider already known by everybody or which are already in disuse, such as *VHS*; and I've also laid aside, for example, more technical words, such as *4K*, related to the image format or quality and which do not contribute much to the understanding of the films or to how they are made.

Neither did I include some words, such as *timing*, which sound like cinema, but which are more widely used terms.

You will probably miss, then, some words or may think that some others are not needed. I apologise if that is the case, but I had to set limits at some points, regarding what to include and what not (for example, this section may result in just an English dictionary)....

A

ADR: Additional Dialogue Replacement. It is the substitution of the dialogues recorded at the time of the shooting by other clearer ones recorded at the studio.

Animatronics: They are puppets with mechanisms to be remotely operated and thus simulate, for instance the white shark at "Jaws".

Anime: It is Japanese animation cinema.

Aspect ratio: It is the proportional relationship between the image's width and height, for example, the common panoramic ratio of 16:9.

Auteur: It is normally used this way for a filmmaker who controls almost everything in his/her films, being often the screenwriter and director.

B

B film: It is a low-budget film which is not usually released in cinemas and go directly to television.

Background: It is the back of a set or scenery in a film.

Biopic: It's a biographical film.

Blaxploitation: It is a cinematographic phenomenon born in the 1970s, which we could define as cinema by and for African Americans.

Blockbuster: It is a film of questionable quality which, nevertheless, achieves great box-office success.

Blooper: It's a mistake made during the shooting.

Bollywood: This is how the film industry based in Mumbai (India) is colloquially known, with a large production but limited impact in the West.

Boom: It's the telescopic stand to support the microphone over the actors.

Breaking the 180-degree rule: Between the characters within a scene there's an imaginary axis defined by their eye gaze direction. To avoid inconsistencies, the 180-degree rule is kept, which implies filming with the camera within the 180 degrees of one of the sides of the axis. This would be better understood with a graphic, but imagine two people looking at each other: when the camera focuses on the one on the left, this one should be looking to the right; when the camera focuses on the one on the right, this one should be looking to the left. If each person was focused from one side of the axis, both of them would appear to the audience as if they were looking to the same side and, this way, the impression that they are looking at each other would be lost.

C

Cameo: It is a brief appearance of a famous person in a film.

Camera angle: It's the tilt of the camera axis in relation to the subject being filmed.

Camera dolly: It's a cart to support and move a camera.

Casting: It's the selection of actors and actresses for the cast of a film. Some directors state that a good casting means having 90% of their work done beforehand, although the remaining 10% is determining.

CGI: Computer-Generated Imagery. It's an application to create computer-generated images.

Chroma Key: It's a technique used to remove a specific colour from an image (usually what surrounds the actors, a background filmed on green or blue) and insert other images instead.

Cinéma vérité: It's a French movement which tends to capture life as it is, hence, the technical requirements for the shooting were also simplified.

CinemaScope: It is a panoramic screen format, almost

two and a half times wider than high (2.35:1 [A square image is 1:1]). During the shooting, a special lens compressed the image laterally, widening the visual field, and when projecting it, it was returned to its normal proportions.

Cinerama: It is a system by which three cameras recorded and then were projected onto a huge and deep screen to cover almost the viewer's whole field of vision.

Cliffhanger: It means situations at the end of a film which create expectation to the viewer to watch the next film in which the dilemma is supposed to be solved.

Colour grading: It is the process of colour harmonising, brightness and contrast in a film.

Costume designer: It is the one who creates and/or chooses the costumes for the characters.

Costumer: It is a company or person that supplies theatrical costumes.

Credits: They are texts shown at the beginning and at the end of a film with the name of the persons involved in its production.

Crossover: It is the union of two films or sagas to become another one.

D

Day for night: It is a technique to simulate night when filming in daylight, by applying filters and/or underexposure, and taking care of other aspects, such as shadow projections.

Diegesis: It is the narrative development of facts.

Dissolve: It is a gradual colour transition of a shot until it fills the whole screen (fade-out), or the other way round (fade-in). It is usually used to change scenery or to indicate a temporary change.

Dogme 95: It's a movement started in 1995 by some Danish directors, such as Lars von Trier, who proposed a more traditional and home-made way of making films, for example, filming with the camera on the shoulder, just in real sets and excluding the use of special effects. It included even more debatable rules than the previous ones, such as not being allowed to add sound after the action or not being allowed to use special artificial light.

E

Easter Eggs: In Anglo-Saxo tradition, during Easter, these eggs are hidden for children to look for and find; and regarding cinema, it involves signs or clues to other films.

Editing: It's the assembly of images.

Ellipsis: It's a jump in time or in space, omitting intermediate steps, but preserving the continuity of the sequence.

Epic film: It's cinema which deals with great deeds and personalities of ancient times.

F

Fake: It is something false. It's a fraud or falsification.

Feature film: According to the American Film Institute and others, it is a film with a running time of more than 60 minutes.

Featurette: It is a medium-length film, in between a short film and a full-length film, sometimes it is a kind of documentary, for instance, about the "behind the scenes" of a film.

Film adaptation: It is the script made from a previous work, generally a literary one.

Film d'auteur: It's a film where the director has a dominant influence.

Film editor: It's the name given to the person who selects shots and combines them into sequences.

Film Noir: It's a genre which comprises the topics of crime and corruption.

Flashback: It's the narrative taken back in time.

Flashforward: It's the narrative taken forward in time.

Flip book: It's a booklet with images, arranged in such a way that, when pages are quickly turned, it gives the sense of animation.

Foley: It's the sound effects that reproduce those "room" sounds which, for some reason, couldn't be registered at the moment of shooting the scene.

Found footage: It's a technique by which part or the whole of the film is presented as if it was discovered material, for example, in a horror film, the alleged video camera recording of a person who died while filming.

Frame: It's a still image.

H

Hyperlink cinema: It is a film with several characters and stories, interwoven at the end.

I

Image noise: It is the graininess of the image.

Independent or Indie film: It is a film made outside the traditional means, such as the major film studios.

Insert: It is an interspersed shot to highlight a certain detail.

Interlock: It is a separate but simultaneous projection of two image and/or sound tracks, for example, for dubbing.

J

Jump cut: It is a cut in which two sequential images are taken from different camera positions.

K

Kinescoping: It is the conversion of images in a digital medium or electric medium to a physical film.

L

Leitmotiv: It is a recurring motif throughout a work.

M

MacGuffin: It is a term coined by Alfred Hitchcock to refer to a narrative element which is presented as prominent to the plot, and may be useful to give continuity to it, but which finally turns out to be a diversionary element or, in any case, of little importance.

Mainstream: It's the predominant thoughts or preferences at a certain point.

Majors: It's the dominating film studios.

Making-of: Also known as "behind-the-scenes", it is a documentary film where the production of the film is shown.

Match cut: It is the continuity between shots, in such a way that there's a sense of sequence.

Melodrama: It is a work with a focus on emotional aspects.

Merchandising: It is the commercialisation of products associated to films, such as T-shirts, figures, etc.

Mockumentary: It is the development of a false story, with the techniques specific to the documentary, to pass it off as true.

Morphing: It is a technique to attain the metamorphosis of a being or an object into another one.

Moviola: It is a device to edit a film and view it.

Multiplex (or Megaplex): It is a film theatre complex with multiple screens.

N

New Wave: *Nouvelle vague.* It is a movement that emerged in France around the middle of the 20th century, which encouraged technical freedom and freedom of expression when making films.

P

Panning: It is the change from one shot to another with a quick camera swivel.

Peplum: It is a genre of films set in the Greco-Roman ancient world.

Prequel: It is a story which precedes the original film.

Product placement: It is the incorporation of brands and/or their products into the film itself for their promotion.

Props: They are elements used for the decoration in a film.

R

Reboot: It is a version of a film, with changes that do not affect the basis of the story.

Red band trailer: It's a trailer with adult content.

Remake: It is a version of a previous film.

Replay: It is the repetition of images immediately after having been shown.

Rhythm: It is the combination of order and speed brought to the action of a film.

Road movie: It is a film which takes place throughout a

road journey.

Rushes (or Dailies): They are the unedited positive prints from the negative made by the laboratory, to quickly verify the work of one day.

S

Scene: It is the moment and place where something happens, generally marked by the entry and exit of actors.

Screwball comedy: It is a crazy comedy.

Script supervisor: The script or continuity supervisor is the person in charge of supervising the visual and storyline continuity of the film, taking also into account that the scenes are not usually recorded in the same order in which they will be finally edited.

Sequel: It is a film emerged from another one and set at a later time.

Sequence: It is a series of scenes of a same story unit being told.

Set: It's an artificial space intended to simulate a real place.

Set dresser: He/she takes care of the organisation of movements and stage effects.

Short film: According to the "American Film Institute" and others, it's a film which has a running time of less than 30 minutes.

SHOT: It is a series of images which form a take unit.
_American shot: It frames the subject from the knees up.
_bird's-eye view: From the top, at a perpendicular angle.
_high angle: It's taken from the camera positioned above the subject being filmed.
_Italian shot: It is an extreme close-up which shows the face from the chin to the forehead.
_low view: It's taken from the camera positioned below the subject being filmed.
_point of view shot: It's taken from the point of view of a subject.
_sequence shot: It is a take filmed in continuity, with no cuts between shots.
_worm's-eye view: the camera is positioned perpendicular to the ground, focusing upwards.

Slapstick: It is a comedy subgenre, characterised by exaggerated physical jokes but without violent consequences.

Slasher: It is a subgenre of horror films which could be described by the name itself.

Soundtrack: It is the music of a film; in general, it refers only to the musical part.

Spaghetti Western: It is a Western film shot in Europe, mainly in Italy and Spain, and which, because of its peculiarities, became a subgenre itself.

Spin-off: It is a film which "takes" a charismatic character from another one, making that character the leading role of the new film.

Splatter film: It is the cinema which focuses on what is bloody and unpleasant.

Split-focus dioptre: It is a technique with a lens by which two different points of focus could be shown in the same image (for example, a close-up and a panoramic), usually one on the left side of the screen and another one on the right.

Spoiler: It is some kind of important detail of a film which, if it is revealed, it could ruin it, at least regarding surprises.

Spoof film: It is a parody film.

Spot: It is an advertising message.

Star system: It is a method in cinema focused on the great stars (actors or actresses).

Step outline: It is the skeleton of a script, where the

scenes are detailed, to be added afterwards to the script itself.

Still photo: It is a photograph of a scenes of the film used for documentary or advertising purposes.

Stop motion: It is something similar to what is done in cartoons, but this term is applied when what is really done is to give an impression of movement with the sequence of still photographs.

Storyboard: It is the graphic script of a film which is used as a support to preview it.

Surround: It is a surrounding sound system with speakers that surround the viewer.

Synopsis: It is a summary of the essence of the film.

T

Tagline: It is an advertising sentence, the slogan of the film.

Teaser: It is a pre-launch trailer, with fragmented information.

Telefilm: It is a film for television which adjusts to the way it is produced; for example, since there are usually advertisements on television, in these films there are usually moments of interest in the points where advertising may be placed, and some plot elements are often repeatedly highlighted so that the viewer does not get lost.

Thriller film: It is a genre which creates suspense and tension in the viewer.

Tour de force: It is a way of saying a "turn of the screw".

Tracking shot: It is the tracking of the subject by means of the camera movement on rails or another system.

Trailer: It is a commercial advertisement for a film with a short edition that informs us about what it is about.

U

Underground: It is a cultural movement oblivious to the prevailing one.

V

Visual gag: It's a comic effect.

VOD: *Video On Demand.* It is a system to have access to videos or television on demand.

Vaudeville: It is a light comedy, with spicy or love intrigues; it usually includes musical numbers.

Voice-over: It is the voice of someone who is not on stage.

W

Western: It is a genre set in the US Old West (19th Century).

Wipe: It's an effect which gradually replaces, in different directions, one image with another.

Z

Z movie: Finally, this is how a film considered really bad is called. It has a very low budget and little care in its making.

THE OSCARS AND OTHER FILM AWARDS

Since the early years of the 20th century, the film industry has gradually settled in Hollywood (a district of Los Angeles City, California), because of its good situation and conditions.

The film industry grew quickly and in 1927 it was decided to regulate it by means of the Academy of Motion Picture Arts and Sciences of Hollywood. Douglas Fairbanks was its first president. On 9 May 1927 the Biltmore Hotel hosted a dinner, chaired by Louis B. Mayer, and the establishment of the awards was proposed.

The production designer Cedric Gibbons designed the sketch of the award: a statuette of a masculine aspect gripping a sword standing on a reel of film with one spoke for each original branch of the Academy (5: producers, directors, writers, actors and technicians). The symbol ended up made of bronze and coated in 24-karat gold, with a height of 34 cm and a weight of 3062 g.

Regarding the origin of the name, curiously, it is not very clear, although it seems that back in 1931 a woman felt like saying that the statuette reminded her of a relative called Oscar, and from then on it has been colloquially called this way. However, it was not until 1934, when Walt Disney won a statuette for "Three Little

Pigs" and showed his appreciation "for having won an Oscar", that that name became massively accepted.

The norms and categories of the awards (there was a time, for example, when some categories were split into Colour and Black-and-White) have gone through multiple changes throughout their history and there may be new changes at any time which may make what is written here seem inaccurate... but the following gives an idea of how they work and we'll see some curiosities:

The members of the Academy are the ones who vote. To become a member of the Academy it is necessary to be invited by the Academy's Board of Governors, who, for that purpose, base themselves on the merits achieved in the film field. The members of the Academy with the right to vote must be in any of the following branches: executives, producers, directors, actors (by far the largest branch by far), writers, cinematographers, production designers, film editors, musicians, short film and feature animation directors, sound technicians, visual effects technicians or public relations. ...

Those films premiered in theatres in Los Angeles between January 1 and December 31 of each year enter competition. If a film has been screened at any other place prior to the theatre, it cannot enter competition. In the case of the Best Foreign Language Film, it is not required to have been released in Los Angeles; only one film is accepted from each country and a special committee designates the nominated ones, which are then voted by the members of the Academy who prove to have watched all of them.

During the month of January each year, a questionnaire is sent to the voters, from where the nominations will come out, so that they can select the best films released the year before; nonetheless: only the specialists of each branch vote (actors are chosen by actors, for instance) except in the case of the "best picture", which is voted by all the members of the Academy. Honorary and special awards are chosen by the Academy's Board of Governors. Special committees are formed for the nominations of documentaries and short films. The votes for the nominations are counted and the latter are announced. Then another questionnaire is sent to choose the winners and, in this case, all the members of the Academy vote and the vote is secret.

All the films are shown at the screening rooms of the Academy itself and they are made available to the voters.

An actor/actress cannot be doubly nominated for the same category (by the way, the production companies are the ones which decide if an actor is available for the leading or supporting role), therefore, he/she will only be eligible for the most voted performance for the nomination in case he/she is presented for more than one film.

The counting of votes and later delivery to the Academy in sealed envelopes is carried out by the company Price Waterhouse Co., whose representative is the only one who knows the winners before the ceremony. The number of votes for each category is not made public.

In the first year, there were only 12 categories plus a special award and the next year just 7! Then they gradually increased. It was not until 1936 that the important categories of supporting actor and actress were created. Not until 1956 did foreign language films enter the competition. And it was not until 2001! that the Oscar for best animated feature film was created.

The first award ceremony hosted films released from 1 August 1927 to 31 July 1928. Both nominees and winners were known on 17 February 1929, although the Oscars were not awarded until May 16, at a dinner held at the Hollywood Roosevelt Hotel.

The Oscars kept on evaluating films released in two years until the ceremony of 1932-1933, when they already considered from 1 August 1932 until 31 December 1933, to finally award a complete whole year from 1934 on.

The current categories are, approximately:

Picture (the award is picked up by the producers and not the directors, although sometimes they are the same), director, actor, actress, supporting actor, supporting actress, original screenplay, adapted screenplay, cinematography, film editing, production design, original score, song, sound, costume design, makeup, visual effects, sound editing, documentary feature, documentary short subject, animated feature film, animated short film, live action short film, foreign language film. /// The scientific and technical Oscars are given separately from the ceremony.

Until 2008 only 5 films were nominated for the best picture, but in 2009 (therefore, for the 2010 ceremony) they were increased to a maximum of 10, with the condition of at least 5% of the votes, for this reason, since then, the number of nominated ones varies from 5 to 10.

OSCAR RECORDS:

	OSCARS won	NOMINATIONS
FILM	11 - The Lord of the Rings: The Return of the King -Titanic -Ben-Hur	14 -La La Land -Titanic -All about Eve
DIRECTOR	4 -John Ford	12 -William Wyler
ACTOR	3 -Daniel Day-Lewis -Jack Nicholson -Walter Brennan	12 -Jack Nicholson
ACTRESS	4 -Katharine Hepburn	21 -Meryl Streep [3 Oscars]
General	26 -Walt Disney	59 -Walt Disney

Among the "losers", we could cite "The Color Purple" (1985) and "The Turning Point" (1977) with 11 nominations each and 0 Oscars.

John Williams, who has 5 Oscars, is the living person with the highest number of nominations (51 times). Furthermore, he is the person who has competed the most times against himself: 2011, 2005, 2001, 1995, 1991, 1989, 1987, 1984, 1977, 1973, 1972 and 1969.

The non-English speaking countries which won the most Oscars for that category are: Italy, with 14 (out of 28 nominations) and France, with 12 (out of 37 nominations). Spain is in the third place, with 4 Oscars out of 19 nominations. Moreover, it must be considered that the French film "The Artist" won the Oscar for Best Picture 2011, in addition to other 4, among a total of 10 nominations, being a silent film (to be precise, at the end of the film a few sentences are said in English).

Only 10 non-English speaking films have been nominated for "best picture": La Grande Illusion (1938. France), Z (1969. France), The Emigrants (1972. Sweden), Cries and Whispers (1973. Sweden), Il Postino (1995. Italy), La Vita è Bella (1998. Italy), Crouching Tiger, Hidden Dragon (2000. Taiwan), Letters from Iwo Jima (2006. US but filmed in Japanese), Amour (2012. Austria) and Roma (2018. Mexico. The only one in the list in Spanish language).

Only seven non-English speaking performances have won the Oscar: Sophia Loren (1961. Best actress), Robert de Niro (1974. Best supporting actor. Por "The Godfather: Part II", his role in Italian), Roberto Benigni (1998. Best actor), Benicio del Toro (2000. Best supporting actor), Marion Cotillard (2007. Best actress), Javier Bardem (2007. Best supporting actor) and

Penélope Cruz (2008. Best supporting actress) who, by the way, would be the first Spanish actress to have a star on the Hollywood Walk of Fame on 1 April 2011.

There has been a tie three times. One at the 1931/31 Oscars, between Fredric March and Wallace Beery for the best actor category, although in fact, March had received one more vote than Beery, but at the time such a small margin of difference was considered a tie. Another one in 1968 between Barbra Streisand and Katharine Hepburn for best actress. And another one in 2012 for the Sound Editing category between the films "Zero Dark Thirty" and "Skyfall".

The sound engineer Kevin O'Connell is the person with the most nominations received without having won any of them: 20... although at the 21st time, that of 2016 (given in 2017, of course) he did win it.

The Irishman Barry Fitzgerald is the only actor to be nominated for both categories (actor and supporting actor) in the same film and the same role. What a nonsense! It was for "Going my Way" in 1944. He won the Oscar for supporting actor.

Steven Spielberg is the producer who has been the most nominated, with 10 of his productions having been nominated for best picture.

"Beauty and the Beast" (Walt Disney) is the only animated feature film to compete for an Oscar in the "best picture" category... until 2008. In 2009 they expanded to 10 nominees for best picture instead of the usual 5 (in 2011 they also added the condition that, in order to be nominated, a film should have had at least 5% of the votes, that year there were 9 nominees for that category), and from then on, also "Up and "Toy Story 3" have been nominated for best animated feature film.

That concludes this review of the most important film awards, leaving below a list with all the winners for best picture, with my modest and *arguable personal assessment, just as a matter of interest, or, if considered appropriate, as a critical reference:

*A single film may be more or less liked, depending on the circumstances in which it is watched... and in the case of some films such as The Lord of the Rings, I've rated it high because of its thorough production, although I barely liked it.

HISTORICAL RECORD of OSCARS for BEST picture

(Best animated feature film in grey)

YEAR	TITLE	DIRECTOR (* IF ALSO OSCAR) PRODUCER	NOMINATIONS / OSCAR	My Rating
2018	Green Book	Peter Farrelly	5/3	7
	Spider-Man: Into the Spider-Verse	Sony / Marvel / *	1/1	4
2017	The Shape of Water	*Guillermo del Toro	13/4	6
	Coco	Pixar Animation Studios / Walt Disney Pictures	2/2	6
2016	Moonlight	Barry Jenkins	8/3	5
	Zootopia	Walt Disney Animation Studios	1/1	6
2015	Spotlight	Thomas McCarthy	6/2	6
	Inside Out	Pixar Animation Studios / Walt Disney Pictures	2/1	5
2014	Birdman or (The Unexpected Virtue of Ignorance)	*Alejandro González Iñárritu	9/4	5

	Big Hero 6	Walt Disney	1 / 1	6
2013	Twelve Years a Slave	Steve McQueen	9/3	5
	Frozen	Walt Disney Pictures	2 / 2	4
2012	Argo	Ben Affleck	7/3	6
	Brave	Pixar	1 / 1	5
2011	The Artist	*Michel Hazanavicius	10/5	8
	Rango	Nickelodeon GK Films - Blind Wink	1 / 1	3
2010	The King´s Speech	*Tom Hooper	12 / 4	5
	Toy Story 3	Pixar	5 / 2	9
2009	The Hurt Locker	*Kathryn Bigelow	9 / 6	7
	Up·	Pixar	5 / 2	8
2008	Slumdog Millionaire	*Danny Boyle	10 / 8	7
	Wall-E	Pixar	6 / 1	6
2007	No Country for Old Men	*Joel & Ethan Coen	8 / 4	4
	Ratatouille	Pixar	5 / 1	7
2006	The Departed	*Martin Scorsese	5 / 4	6
	Happy Feet	Warner Bros Village Roadshow	1 / 1	7
2005	Crash	Paul Haggis	6 / 3	7
	Wallace & Gromit: The Course of the Were-Rabbit	DreamWorks Aardman Animation	1 / 1	7
2004	Million Dollar Baby	*Clint Eastwood	7 / 4	6

	The Incredibles	*Pixar*	*4 / 2*	*9*
2003	The Lord of the Kings. The Return of the King	*Peter Jackson	11 / 11	7
	Finding Nemo	*Pixar*	*5 / 1*	*9*
	Chicago	Rob Marshall	13 / 6	6
2002	*Spirited Away (Sen to Chihiro no Kamigakure)*	*Studio Ghibli*	*3 / 2*	*4*
2001	A Beautiful Mind	*Ron Howard	8 / 4	7
	Shrek	*DreamWorks*	*2 / 1*	*8*
2000	Gladiator	Ridley Scott	12 / 5	8
1999	American Beauty	*Sam Mendes	8 / 5	7
1998	Shakespeare in Love	John Madden	12 / 7	6
1997	Titanic	*James Cameron	14 / 11	9
1996	The English Patient	*Anthony Minghella	12 / 9	4
1995	Braveheart	*Mel Gibson	10 / 5	10
1994	Forrest Gump	*Robert Zemeckis	13 / 6	10
1993	**Schindler´s List**	***Steven Spielberg**	12 / 7	**10**

1992	Unforgiven	*Clint Eastwood	9 / 4	6
1991	The Silence of the Lambs	*Jonathan Demme	7 / 5	6
1990	Dances with Wolves	*Kevin Costner	12 / 7	8
1989	Driving Miss Daisy	Bruce Beresford	9 / 4	5
1988	Rain Man	*Barry Levinson	8 / 4	5
1987	The Last Emperor	*Bernardo Bertolucci	9 / 9	5
1986	Platoon	*Oliver Stone	8 / 4	6
1985	Out of Africa	*Sidney Pollack	11 / 7	3
1984	Amadeus	*Milos Forman	11 / 8	4
1983	Terms of Endearment	*James L. Brooks	11 / 5	6
1982	Gandhi	*Richard Attenborough	11 / 8	8
1981	Chariots of Fire	Hugh Hudson	7 / 4	7
1980	Ordinary People	*Robert Redford	6 / 4	5
1979	Kramer vs.	*Robert	9 / 5	7

	Kramer	*Benton*		
1978	*The Deer Hunter*	**Michael Cimino*	*9 / 5*	*5*
1977	*Annie Hall*	**Woody Allen*	*5 / 4*	*5*
1976	*Rocky*	**John G. Avildsen*	*10 / 3*	*6*
1975	*One Flew Over the Cuckoo´s Nest*	**Milos Forman*	*9 / 5*	*8*
1974	*The Godfather Part II*	**Francis Ford Coppola*	*11 / 6*	*7*
1973	*The Sting*	**George Roy Hill*	*10 / 7*	*8*
1972	*The Godfather*	**Francis Ford Coppola*	*11 / 3*	*9*
1971	*The French Connection*	**William Friedkin*	*8 / 5*	*5*
1970	*Patton*	**Franklin J. Shaffner*	*10 / 7*	*8*
1969	*Midnight Cowboy*	**John Schlesinger*	*7 / 3*	*4*
1968	*Oliver!*	**Carol Reed*	*11 / 6*	*6*
1967	*In the Heat of the Night*	*Norman Jewison*	*7 / 5*	*6*
1966	*A Man for All Seasons*	**Fred Zinnemann*	*8 / 6*	*3*
1965	*The Sound of Music*	**Robert Wise*	*10 / 5*	*4*
1964	*My Fair Lady*	**George Cukor*	*12 / 8*	*2*
1963	*Tom Jones*	**Tony Richardson*	*10 / 4*	*4*
1962	*Lawrence of Arabia*	**David Lean*	*10 / 7*	*7*
1961	*West Side Story*	**Robert Wise & Jerome*	*11 / 10*	*4*

		Robbins		
1960	The Apartment	*Billy Wilder	10 / 5	8
1959	Ben-Hur	*William Wyler	12 / 11	7
1958	Gigi	*Vincente Minnelli	9 / 9	4
1957	The Bridge on the River Kwai	*David Lean	8 / 7	7
1956	Around the World in Eighty Days	Michael Anderson	8 / 5	5
1955	Marty	*Delbert Mann	8 / 4	5
1954	On the Waterfront	*Elia Kazan	12 / 8	7
1953	From Here to Eternity	*Fred Zinnemann	13 / 8	5
1952	The Greatest Show on Earth	Cecil B. De Mille	5 / 2	7
1951	An American in Paris	Vincente Minnelli	8 / 6	3
1950	All About Eve	*Joseph L. Mankiewicz	14 / 6	7
1949	All the King´s Men	Robert Rossen	7 / 3	5
1948	Hamlet	Laurence Olivier	7 / 4	6
1947	Gentleman´s Agreement	*Elia Kazan	8 / 3	7
1946	The Best Years of Our Lives	*William Wyler	9 / 8	7
1945	The Lost Weekend	*Billy Wilder	7 / 4	6
1944	Going My Way	*Leo McCarey	10 / 7	4
1943	Casablanca	*Michael Curtiz	8 / 3	8
1942	Mrs. Miniver	*William	12 / 6	4

		Wyler		
1941	How Green Was My Valley	*John Ford	10 / 5	3
1940	Rebecca	Alfred Hitchcock	11 / 2	6
1939	Gone with the Wind	*Victor Fleming	13 / 8	7
1938	You Can´t Take It with You	*Frank Capra	7 / 2	7
1937	The Life of Emile Zola	William Dieterle	10 / 3	8
1936	The Great Ziegfeld	Robert Z. Leonard	7 / 3	4
1935	Mutiny on the Bounty	Frank Lloyd	8 / 1	6
1934	It Happened One Night	*Frank Capra	5 / 5	7
1932/33	Cavalcade	*Frank Lloyd	4 / 3	4
1931/32	Grand Hotel	Edmond Goulding	1 / 1	4
1930/31	Cimarron	Wesley Ruggles	7 / 3	5
1929/30	All Quiet on the Western Front	*Lewis Milestone	4 / 2	5
1928/29	The Broadway Melody	Harry Beaumont	3 / 1	3
1927/28	Wings	William A. Wellman	2 / 2	6

The lists of awards, although the latter may have been influenced by trends or clear injustices, might be themselves recommendations of films "to be watched", therefore I refer you also to other lists which you can easily find on the internet, of other important awards, such as the Golden Globes (bestowed by the Hollywood Foreign Press Association since 1944; although in 1952 they split the best picture category into two: Best drama picture & Best comedy or musical picture), the Spanish Goyas (since 1987), the British BAFTAs, the French Césars, etc... in addition to the great film festivals, such as that of Cannes (France), Berlin (Germany), Venice (Italy), San Sebastián (Spain), Rome (Italy), Sundance (US), etc.

I cannot leave without making a reference to the bibliography consulted for this book.

Nevertheless, to do so is a problem.

It is so much and, in some cases, for so few (from some books I have only taken one detail)... that it is simply impossible for me to depict everything.

Moreover, some of these consultations are from years ago and I have recovered them from notes in my modest website about cinema: cinefilia.com.es, so I don't remember the original source... although in most cases there could have been several sources.

In any case, I should point out at least a book which has served as a basis for the sections "A brief history of cinema" and "Who is who? – How a film is made". This is the book "El Cine" [Cinema] by the publishing house Larousse (2009).

Regarding the Oscars, I do remember that the book I served as a basis at the moment was "Enciclopedia de los Oscar" [Oscars Encyclopaedia], by Luis Miguel Carmona (T&B Editores, 2006)... and also the work in instalments "Todos los Oscars" [All the Oscars], by José Luis Mena (Cacitel S. L.).

There are many other books which have barely contributed to this one, but which are very good and I want to recommend one to you: "Lecciones de cine [Moviemakers' Masterclass]", by Laurent Tirard (Paidós, 2003).

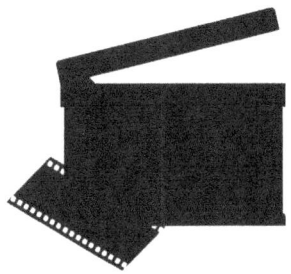

Book finished on 28 April 2019, in Folgoso de la Ribera (Leon - Spain)

Translated from the Spanish version by
Cristina Sánchez Moralejo
(Year 2021)

www.ingramcontent.com/pod-product-compliance
Lightning Source LLC
Chambersburg PA
CBHW070406220526
45467CB00001B/493